D1101235

9112000238711

Plant Life

SEED SAFARI

Judith Heneghan and Diego Moscato

WAYLAND

First published in 2015 by Wayland
Copyright © Wayland 2015

Wayland
338 Euston Road
London NW1 3BH

Wayland Australia
Level 17/207 Kent Street
Sydney, NSW 2000

All rights reserved

Editor: Nicola Edwards
Design: Anthony Hannant, Little Red Ant

A catalogue record for this title is available from the British Library.
Dewey: 581.4'67-dc23
ISBN 978 0 7502 8763 0
Library e-book ISBN: 978 0 7502 8764 7

Printed in China

Wayland, part of Hachette Children's Group and published by
Hodder and Stoughton Limited
www.hachette.co.uk

BRENT LIBRARIES	
KIL	
91120000238711	
Askews & Holts	22-Apr-2015
J581.467 JUNIOR NON-	£11.99

Contents

All around the world, plants grow in amazing variety. Each plant has the same goal: to spread its seeds so that they can grow into new plants. Read on to discover the wonderful ways in which different seeds reach their own patch of earth.

On a beach in southern India, coconut palms are swaying.
A ripe coconut, green and heavy, falls with a thud to the shore.
A wave lifts it up and carries it out to sea. The coconut drifts
on strong ocean currents. It will never return to the beach
where it first grew.

A coconut is a type of fruit. It contains a single seed. In the right conditions, seeds germinate and grow into new plants. A new plant needs plenty of light and water and food, so each seed must move away from the parent plant to avoid overcrowding.

After long weeks at sea, the coconut washes up on a distant shore. Its thick skin has rotted but it still has its brown shell. There's plenty of light here, and space to grow. Soon the seed within the shell sends out a green shoot. Its journey is over.

A coconut is large and heavy, but it doesn't sink because it has a hollow centre. Its thick skin and tough shell help protect the seed inside from the salty sea water. It is perfectly adapted for floating across an ocean.

The coconut may travel up to 2000 miles before it reaches land.

Other plants also spread their seeds by water. The monkey ladder vine produces long, twisting seed pods that dangle from the trees. As the pods dry, they split open. The shiny, heart-shaped seeds fall into streams and rivers that wash them out to sea. Some people call the seeds 'sea beans'.

A bean is a kind of seed. There are many types of sea bean, but all have a hard shell and a hollow space inside that keeps them afloat. Sea beans have been known to cross the Atlantic Ocean.

9

The seeds of the Jacaranda have a thin, papery rim. A broad, flat surface helps to keep them airborne in a breeze.

Water isn't the only way to travel. Many seeds float through the air. These seeds are small and light. They may have feathery tufts or fine hairs or be as tiny as specks of dust. Some seeds will glide for a short distance. Others may be swept up by strong winds and carried over mountain ranges or wafted across continents.

Each tiny cattail seed is attached to several long, fine hairs. When the cattail seed pod opens, thousands of seeds blow away in a cloud of light fluff.

And what of the beautiful field maple tree? Each seed has two papery wings. In the autumn these seeds fall away from the parent tree. Some say they twirl like pirouetting ballerinas. Others say they whirl like helicopters.

The seeds of the sycamore and ash trees also have delicate wings that help carry them through the air.

Some seed pods don't wait
for the wind to disperse their
precious contents.
Instead they dry out in
the sun. As they dry, they
become tight and brittle until
suddenly they split open,
flinging out their seeds.

When the pumpkin-sized seed pod of the Sandbox Tree bursts, it hurls its seeds up to one hundred metres across the rainforest. Don't stand too close! The explosion echoes loudly through the undergrowth. For this reason, the Sandbox Tree is sometimes called the Dynamite Tree.

15

The seeds of the wild oat plant move all by themselves. Each seed has an outer case with a long hair or bristle. The bristle is bent in the middle. When the seed falls to the ground, it waits for a drop of moisture to soften its bristle and straighten it. This causes the seed to roll over.

As the bristle dries out, it bends back again. In this way the seed keeps rolling until it finds a dark, damp hollow. Now it can germinate safely.

The wild oat is often seen as a weed. It spreads quickly because it is so perfectly adapted to finding a safe place to germinate and grow.

17

Some seeds don't need to travel away from the parent plant. The seeds of the Jack Pine Tree are stored in tight cones. These cones open and drop their seeds in extreme heat only — the heat of a forest fire. The fire kills the parent tree, but the seeds survive. They fall into the ashes and send up shoots to repopulate the forest.

The ash that is left after a fire
is full of nutrients. It provides
the perfect environment for the
germinating seeds.

Many seeds rely on animals to help them find a new home.
They hitch a ride as the animal brushes past, fastening
themselves to paws or catching on fur or sticking to
beaks and feathers.

The seed case of the burdock plant is
called a 'burr'. The burr is covered with
spikes that have tiny hooks at the end.
When these hooks catch on an animal's
fur, they are difficult to shake off. The
animal may have to carry that seed case
for several days.

The seeds of the broadleaf plantain, when damp with dew or rain, produce a sticky jelly that helps them stick to fur or feathers.

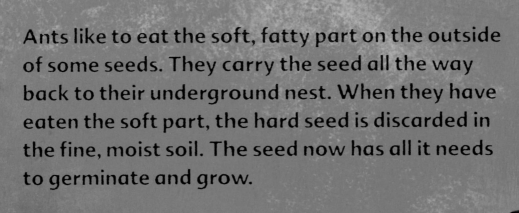

Ants like to eat the soft, fatty part on the outside of some seeds. They carry the seed all the way back to their underground nest. When they have eaten the soft part, the hard seed is discarded in the fine, moist soil. The seed now has all it needs to germinate and grow.

Some animals will even dig a hole for a nut, which is a type of seed. Squirrels collect nuts and bury them in soft earth to eat later. They may come back for them — but not always!

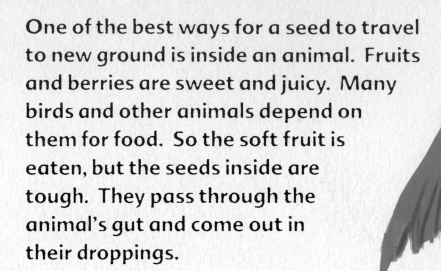

One of the best ways for a seed to travel to new ground is inside an animal. Fruits and berries are sweet and juicy. Many birds and other animals depend on them for food. So the soft fruit is eaten, but the seeds inside are tough. They pass through the animal's gut and come out in their droppings.

Fruits need to look colourful or smell strongly to tempt animals to eat them. The durian, or king of fruits grows in the forests of Malaysia. Orang-utans can sniff its powerful, rotting scent from up to one kilometre away!

An animal's droppings are rich in nutrients, ideal for germination.

People are very good at transporting seeds to new ground. Wheat, rice, fruit, beans and nuts — all are planted and picked and carried to market. Many are eaten, but some will be planted and watered and tended until they have new fruits and seeds of their own.

Others may fall by the wayside.

And a few seeds, like these dandelion seeds, are given a little extra help on their journey to a new patch of earth.

Glossary

adapted — developed special features in order to survive and thrive

disperse — scatter

endangered — under threat

germinate — when a seed develops a root and a shoot — the first stage of life for a new plant

repopulate — young plants allowed to grow

seed pod — the outer case inside which lots of individual seeds develop

species — different types of plants or animals

Further information

There are lots of fascinating plants with clever means of seed dispersal that have not been mentioned in this book. See what you can find out about the following:

- The devil's claw plant
- The birdcage plant
- The whirling gyrocarpus
- The geranium

The Millennium Seed Bank in Kew, London, is a place where seeds are stored to make sure that endangered plants do not become extinct. It aims to hold seeds for one quarter of the world's wild plant species by 2020. You can find out more about its work, and why saving seeds is so important, by visiting http://www.kew.org/science-conservation/millennium-seed-bank.

Things to do

Go on a seed safari! Take a walk through a field or along a hedgerow or into a wood and see how many different seeds you can find. In summer they will be forming on the plant. In the autumn they will be dispersing, and in the winter you'll see some on the ground. You may have to look quite hard in the spring!

Look out especially for the following:

- Conkers (from the horse chestnut tree)
- Sycamore helicopters
- Beech nuts
- Apples
- Berries
- Grass seeds
- Old Man's Beard

Index